This is my family

Bobbie Kalman

 Crabtree Publishing Company

www.crabtreebooks.com

Created by Bobbie Kalman

Author and Editor-in-Chief
Bobbie Kalman

Educational consultants
Reagan Miller
Elaine Hurst
Joan King

Editors
Joan King
Reagan Miller
Kathy Middleton

Proofreader
Crystal Sikkens

Design
Bobbie Kalman
Katherine Berti

Photo research
Bobbie Kalman

Production coordinator
Katherine Berti

Prepress technician
Katherine Berti

Photographs
Bobbie Kalman: p. 3 (bottom left), 8, 10 (right)
Other photographs by Shutterstock

Library and Archives Canada Cataloguing in Publication

Kalman, Bobbie, 1947-
     This is my family / Bobbie Kalman.

(My world)
ISBN 978-0-7787-9432-5 (bound).--ISBN 978-0-7787-9476-9 (pbk.)

     1. Families--Juvenile literature.
I. Title. II. Series: My world (St. Catharines, Ont.)

HQ519.K34 2010   j306.85   C2009-906067-1

Library of Congress Cataloging-in-Publication Data

Kalman, Bobbie.
   This is my family / Bobbie Kalman.
       p. cm. -- (My world)
   ISBN 978-0-7787-9476-9 (pbk. : alk. paper) -- ISBN 978-0-7787-9432-5
(reinforced library binding : alk. paper)
   1. Families--Juvenile literature. I. Title. II. Series.

HQ519.K355 2010
306.85--dc22

                                                  2009041184

Crabtree Publishing Company

www.crabtreebooks.com   1-800-387-7650

Printed in China/122009/CT20091009

Published in Canada
Crabtree Publishing
616 Welland Ave.
St. Catharines, Ontario
L2M 5V6

Published in the United States
Crabtree Publishing
PMB 59051
350 Fifth Avenue, 59th Floor
New York, New York 10118

Published in the United Kingdom
Crabtree Publishing
Maritime House
Basin Road North, Hove
BN41 1WR

Published in Australia
Crabtree Publishing
386 Mt. Alexander Rd.
Ascot Vale (Melbourne)
VIC 3032

Words to know

adopted   divorced   grandfather
              stepmother   grandparent

grandmother

quadruplets   triplets   twins

Families are different.
Some families are small.
I have a small family.
My family is my mother,
father, and me.

I have a big family.

My family has seven people.

How many children are there?

5

My brother and I are **twins**.
We were born on the same day.
Some twins look alike, but my
brother and I do not look the same.

My three sisters are **triplets**.

They were born on the same day.

They are younger than I am.

I am older than they are.

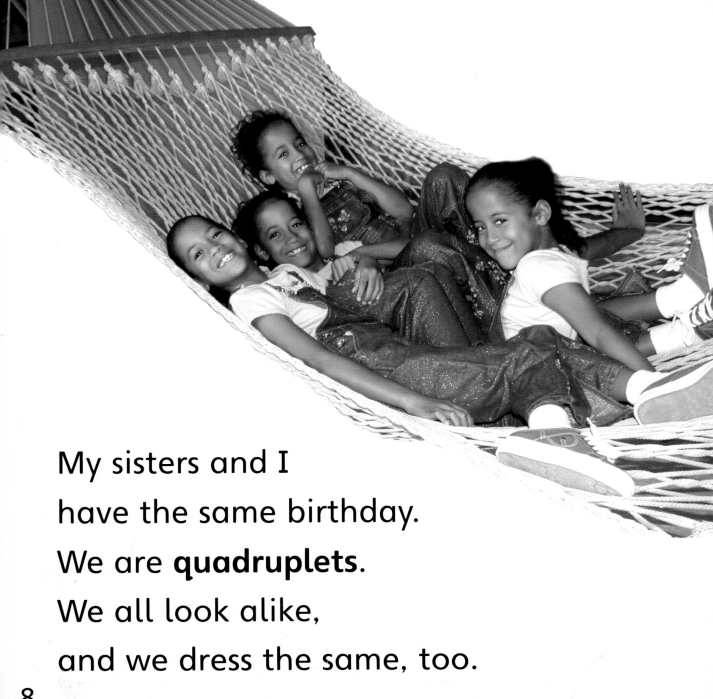

My sisters and I
have the same birthday.
We are **quadruplets**.
We all look alike,
and we dress the same, too.

My sister and I were **adopted**.
We have an older brother.
We are a very happy family.

We love our **grandparents**!
My **grandfather** tells us
stories about our family.
He shows us old family pictures.

My **grandmother** is teaching us how to bake. She bakes the best muffins! We eat them all.

My mother and father are **divorced**.
We live with our mother half the time.
We live with our father half the time.
We love both our parents.

My parents are divorced.
I have a **stepmother**.
She helps take care of us.

Who are the people in your family?
How do you have fun together?
What games do you play?

Activity

Write a book about your family.

Write some funny or happy stories.

Put some family pictures into your book.

Notes for adults

Different kinds of families
This is my family introduces siblings such as twins, triplets, quadruplets, and family situations such as divorce and adoption. Other family situations that could be introduced, if appropriate, are parents that have died or are serving in a war. Ask the children about their families. Are their families the same or different from the families of their friends? How many siblings or cousins do they have? Do they have grandparents? What do they like most about them? How would they like being one of triplets or quadruplets?

Make a family tree
Have the children make their own family tree, using family photographs or drawings. Remind them that not everyone's family tree will look the same and that every tree is special. This reminder will help children be more sensitive to different family situations (single-parents, only children, foster-parents, or unwed parents). When the children complete their family trees, ask them to "introduce" their families using the family vocabulary from the book. This activity will allow them to practice using important "family" words. It also provides a visual representation of different family units.

Being kind to family members
Have the children brainstorm ideas of how they can be good daughters/sons, sisters/brothers, or grandchildren. How can they be kind to their family members? How can they show them how much they love them?